Random Poetry

Synonym Poetry

Caring

Sharing, promoting, loving,
All these qualities are supporting.

Music

Motioning, relieving, connecting,
It is most definitely relaxing.

~Marquonda Wyatt

Author's Biography & A Note from the Author

Marquonda Wyatt is an American Businesswoman, Entrepreneur, Innovator, Author, Writer, Poet, and a Michigan native, thus, an alumni and MBA student attending the University of Michigan. She exudes an immense passion for writing. I have written this book in acknowledgment of the encouragement and enrichment of lives as well as an expression of my own creativity in the world of poetry. In the current lifetime where things are interchangeable yet dynamic while witnessing some ebbs and flows in the world view, the messages are present for the reminder to increase the idea of a positive outlook to facilitate one's journey throughout life as well as the awareness of recent events that's occurring within the world we live in.

Marquonda Wyatt would like to dedicate and deliver a special thank you to her exquisite Parents, Mary and Marvin Wyatt for their continuous and relentless support.

Table of Contents

Author's Biography & A Note from the Author……………Preface

Random Poetry

Synonym Poetry……………………………………………………1
Rules for the Moon……………………………………………...2
From Our Heavenly Lord Above…………………………......3
The Poem of Encouragement…………………………………4
Self-Esteem……………………………………………………...5
POELitical Moments (Political Moments)…………………6
In Technological Times……………………………………......7
The New Millennial……………………………………………..8

Inspirational Poetry

Boss Lady Anthem…………………………………………….11
The View from the Top…………………..…………………...12
The Road to Success……………….………..……………….13
Gracing in Style…………………………………………….....14
Peace of Mind…………………………………………………15
Good Times……………………………………..…………….16
Goals and Challenges……………………………......……..17
Real Beauty……………………………………………………18
A Silver lining…………………………………………………19
Smile……………………………………………………..…....20
Synergy……………………………………………………….21
Strength………………………………………………………22
Staying Strong……………………………………………….23
A Tale of a Leader………………………………….………..24
The American Dream…………..…………………….……..25
The Variations of Love………………...…………….……..26
Credits and Copyrights………………………………….….27

Rules for the Moon

1. Contains light and keep bright.
2. Stay up 'til morning and night.
3. Always contains glow.
4. At sunrise you will be low.
5. When it's your time up you will go.

~Marquonda Wyatt

From Our Heavenly Lord Above

From our Heavenly Lord above,

He is love,

Through every warfare he is strong, mighty, and tough,

What a fixed fight so put on your gloves.

With his mercy and grace,

This is something we can not phase,

So we lift our hands up and praise,

That's what I say,

Get up and pray.

Always keep the faith,

Miracles and blessings granted that we can't calculate.

A phenomenon that we can't explain,

All from the almighty and great.

So watch out the King of Kings,

The Lord of Lords,

His blood and his covering will remain to soar,

From our Heavenly Lord above.

~Marquonda Wyatt

The Poem of Encouragement

Be the best you can be,

Do the best you can do,

Because no one can control anyone's actions but you.

Do all of the following your dreams will come true,

Then you may lead to your moment of truth.

~Marquonda Wyatt

Self-Esteem

Self-Esteem

Sweeter than cream,

The ingredient to succeed,

The energy that you feed,

The quality that you need.

Know what you mean,

With yourself you will come clean,

Be aware that everything is not what it seems,

Be the best version of you that gleams,

Be that team player that everyone can come and lean.

Find your own happy,

Leading to plea,

Then you'll spread your wings and flee,

I hope that you realize and see,

View that bright sunrise beam.

~Marquonda Wyatt

POELitical Moments (Political Moments)

Taking a glimpse into our political world,
A concoction of chaos and swirls,
Such a subjective field,
With crazy whims.

Upcoming elections,
The votes and rejections.
The lies and foes,
The manipulated ballets and polls.

The greed and corruption,
The distractions and infections,
The insurrections and progressions,
The pandemic's inception and mental health mishappen.

Inflation arises,
Stock markets and interest rates collides,
Recession, resignation approaches and uprise,
The Russian and Ukrainian war with Citizen cries.

~Marquonda Wyatt

In Technological Times

Absorbed in technology can be really rewiring,
Seeing all of the trends and all of the money.

The money we spend, technology increases,
Companies get rich, prepare for your brain to get quenched.

Tech gadgets releasing left and right,
Consumers work hard to purchase with all their might.

Spending several hours on the phone and computer,
Maintenance is necessary, how about a troubleshooter.

This tool that's digitally and rapidly advanced,
 Virtual reality will have you in a trance.

All of the newest attributes and features,
All happening before our eyes faster than a meter.

A helpful resource that has come to be,
What are we ever going to need?

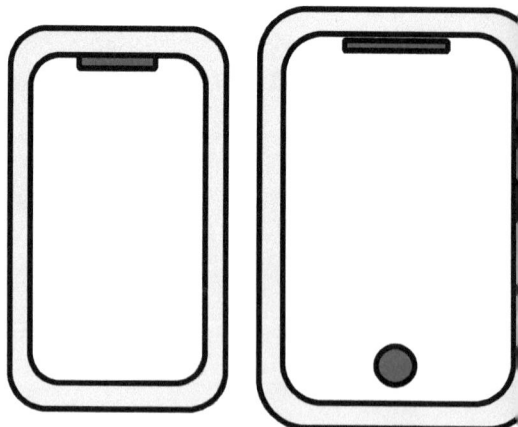

As we progress in modern times,
The best is definitely yet to thrive.

~Marquonda Wyatt

The New Millennial

In these dashing and trying times,
We still have a chance to certainly rise,
Persevere through the deceptive lies.

The infatuation with digital applications,
The urge of instant gratification,
For the generic route of satisfaction.

God will arrive soon, the resurrection,
Repent and improve your imperfections,
Be in sync and have a connection.

The frequent conflicts with the election,
Youngsters driving very reckless,
The vast costs of current taxes.

The ailments that disperse,
The vaccinations becoming diverse,
Selective stubborn Citizens making it worse.

The rain, the storms;
The continuous wars,
 It rains, it pours.

The great resignation,
The plummeting patience,
Employers and Employees no longer having any relation.

The pitiful school and public shootings,
Copycats attempt it as a rebooting,
Many Parents and Guardians are suing.

The Supreme Court ruling,
Misinformation, who do you think the news is fooling?
Climate change, global warming, the earth's core is cooling.

Government of the corrupt,
Interests rates a complete rut,
Better wish us luck.

~**Marquonda Wyatt**

The New Millennial

The appetite for greed and power,
The weak, the coward;
The money towers.

People do what they see,
This can come with a fee,
Who knows what it will lead.

Social media obsession,
Becoming a systemic oppression,
Understand the lesson.

The irony and misconceptions,
The pressure to make impressions,
The wandering confessions.

Student loan forgiveness,
The closing of a business,
Employment rates in the zone of redness.

Inflation rates yet financial crisis,
The smoke and mirrors that entice us,
Oh, the crazy horizons.

Violence and hate,
The phony and fake,
Rely on your innate.

Prejudice and racism,
The political fascism,
Full of masochism.

~**Marquonda Wyatt**

The New Millennial

The need for affordable housing,
The disguises that seems arousing,
The pollution continues to appear piling.

Control over women's and abortion rights,
Not going anywhere without a fight,
Protests are rolling on tight.

President under pressure,
How's he handling all of the stressors?
Putting the doubt on the dresser.

Healthcare workers are overwhelmed,
Working days and nights,
What a slam.

Skeptical of conspiracies,
The Government's ascendency,
The multiple contingencies.

Black Lives Matter,
The public chatter,
Pockets of the rich gets fatter.

In this world we can defeat,
Improve and peace is what we want to keep,
On this journey and incredible feat.

~**Marquonda Wyatt**

Welcome to the Next Level……..

Prepare to be Inspired.

The Boss Lady Anthem

A boss lady strides,
Stay strong and never cry,
Prosper and fly,
Be aware of the sly,
Hold your head up high,
Get your piece of the pie,
 Manage your time.

Donning the dapper suit with a nice little coupe,
An important meeting with the group,
Making it rain and breaking chains,
Now, that's what I call innovate.
Work hard and here comes the play,
 The queen is officially here to stay.

Think strategically,
Currency flows in so feasibly;
Remember to invest very reasonably,
This is what it's meant to be.

Dreams do come true,
 If you stay true to you,
Do what you have to do,
Avoid the forbidden fruit,
Go hard and you'll have the clue,
Envision and in your hands you'll have the world to rule.

Keep it classy and never trashy,
Ms. CEO, they'll see you flexing.

~Marquonda Wyatt

Glamorous galore,
The roses of war.

The View from the Top

They say it's lonely at the top,
    But stay strong like a rock,
        Knock them out of their socks,
        Never put yourself in a box,
            Chilling on the yachts.

        As you enjoy the view,
            Getting to the cue,
            The realest is categorized in a few.
              The landing is on the moon;
            You'll reach your destination soon.

                Keep moving forward,
                  On the ultimate goal you're going toward,
                    Stay occupied and don't get bored,
                      Stay in your means of what you can afford,
                        Don't always believe the lure,
                      Be yourself and don't jump aboard.

                          ~Marquonda Wyatt

The Road to Success

The drive to succeed,
The initiative to lead,
Jumping in the driver's seat,
Standing on your own two feet,
Visualize what you'll be.

The passion of success,
The desire to be the best,
Stand out from the rest,
Never settle for anything less,
Determination is what to possess.

Be humble to the guests,
Always continue to look what's next,
No rush, take your time, no need to go fast,
Life is like a test,
Celebrate it like it's a fest.

Commitment and devotion,
Accelerate in motions,
Keep your mind open,
Cherish the moment,
Prioritize what's important.

Consistency is key,
Keep your eyes open and see,
The answer to life's meaning,
13 The truth will set you free.

~Marquonda Wyatt

Gracing in Style

Passion for fashion,
A style so posh, spark your imagination,
The dress, the shirt,
The chic leather skirt.

Strut that look,
Swag that will have you shook,
Stiletto on the foot,
Appearing like a model in a magazine book.

Apparel so swank like it's fashion week,
So clean, so pristine, it doesn't need a tweak,
Heads turning, silence, there's not a peep,
The latest trends is what we seek.

~Marquonda Wyatt

Peace of Mind

Sitting on the beach,
So peaceful with no screech,
Smiling through your teeth,
Sand between your toes and feet.

Relaxation and meditation,
These feelings you're catching,
Your soul and serenity matching,
No worries and latching.

Self-care is a must,
Remind yourself of trust,
That delicate touch,
All of the above is a wonderful plus.

Peace is a great gift to have,
So join this serendipitous path,
Life is too short for immense wrath,
Express a smile and burst a laugh.

~Marquonda Wyatt

Good Times

Throw your hands up and rejoice,
Stand up tall and lift your voice,
Display confidence and be poise,
Embrace who you are and make some noise.

Who doesn't love a good time,
Joy is such a lovely prime,
While examining this cool rhyme,
Up that hill you will climb.

Viewing what's right,
The field of sight,
Keeping your circle tight,
Witnessing upon the light.

This wonderful concept called life,
Show no weakness and strife,
Keep your head up high like a kite,
And have yourself a good night.

~Marquonda Wyatt

Goals and Challenges

Everyone has a dream,
　　The road that was seen,
　　　　Spilling the tea,
　Following your creed.

　　　　Never run a way from a challenge,
　　　　　　Stay real and don't turn into a savage.
　　　　　　　　The bumps and turns, the tricky crevice,
　　　　Persistence is the formula to leverage.

　　　　　　　　Reaching your destiny,
　　　　　　　　　Preventing blasphemy.
~Marquonda Wyatt~　　　　Oh, what an epiphany,
　　　　　　　Energy arose like a symphony.

　　　　No matter your craft,
　　　　Refine it like a draft.
　　　　Knowing thy self,
　　　　Put the nonsense on the shelf.

Real Beauty

What is real beauty?
Beauty is looked upon as an externality,
But does not last for eternity.
It can be considered vain,
Make people obsessive and insane,
Unrealistic standards to obtain.

Surpassing the vanity wall,
The greatest of it all,
Is the inner self.
In which the authentic beauty crawls,
This is when it never falls,
So stand up tall.

Let your beauty radiate from inside,
Refrain from letting it hide,
Stop wasting time.
Beauty comes from being kind,
As you examine, they will align,
Positivity is a long-term sign.

Swallow the pride,
Allow the real you shine,
Don't look back and leave the old things behind.
Just believe everything will be fine,
Stay in your line,
Be grateful of the things that God has given you in reply.   ~Marquonda Wyatt

A Silver Lining

Defining a silver lining,

Could it be work ethic declining?

Nepotism at its finest.

An opportunity to seize,

A thorough interesting scheme,

A prize to redeem.

Is it all about timing?

Soul searching and finding,

Having your stars aligning.

Is it all about who you know?

Knowing where to flow,

Having your ducks in a row.

Having a deal on a silver platter,

Interpreting the real matter,

Moving up the ladder.

Just know there is hope,

Learn how to cope,

Don't slide into a slope.

Expect the unexpected,

Do you stand corrected?

Look to a prospective. ~Marquonda Wyatt

Smile

That stunning expression,
That helps keep good feelings in a progression,
An attitude that's presented in a good fashion.

It's good for your health and brain,
Keeps you happy and sane,
A frown you would intend to restrain.

Take in the positive vibes,
Life's journey and rides,
The best of both worlds collides.

A smile can go a long way,
A thing that's so contagious,
A good triggering emotion that's outrageous.

The release of endorphins,
A prevention of mood erosions,
A wonderful notion.

Whip up that smile,
We can see it from a mile,
You'll see the results instantly and not in a while.

~Marquonda Wyatt

Synergy

The synonym for energy,
                Goes on 'til infinity,
    Momentum and agility.

    Exists in reality,
Infuses a calorie,
      This is no fallacy.

        Synergy can come in different forms,
                Affects temperatures of cold and warm,
      The principle we need in order to perform.

      The atmospheric matter,
Earth's formation, it's such a flatter,
      Analyzing the latter.

      The energy we give in,
          Determines the win,
    The decisions we intend.

            ~Marquonda Wyatt

Strength

So much emphasis on the physical,
Muscles appearing visible,
The moments that are whimsical.

The strength of your mind,
Will do you very kind,
As you relax and unwind.

The power to persevere,
Through the times that are full of fear,
Only through great will.

The need to stay strong,
Will do you no wrong,
Sing your own song.

Realizing your calling,
It will protect you from falling,
Ignore the ones whose stalling.

~Marquonda Wyatt

Staying Strong

                                                The strong will prevail,
                                                The emotions that are being felt,
                                                Never bow down and kneel.

                The nations stride for improvement,
                  Hear the uproar movement,
                  Start the recruitment.

    In the modern and digital times,
    Where time consistently flies,
     We ask what is the reason why?

 The need for fulfillment,
Stray away from concealment,
 Good vibes keep it reeling.

Just a little note,
Try to stay afloat,
Acknowledge that you're the GOAT (Greatest of All Time).

                                                ~Marquonda Wyatt

A Tale of a Leader

A leader...

Is an efficient people reader,

Be there when others need them.

Assess the route,

Manage the clout,

Results is what they mount.

Provide room for projections,

Proofread for corrections,

The task of data collections.

When things shift to havoc and wreck,

Making the comeback,

Put things back in gear and in full effect.

In case you didn't know,

To cross the threshold,

Do not ever fold.

~Marquonda Wyatt

The American Dream

Fruit of the labor,
The deal on the table,
The outcomes that come later.

The pearl, the lux,
The red bottoms, the clutch,
The sharp black tux,
The Rolex, the blush,
The fine green bucks.

The desire, the wants,
The fabricated fronts,
The drive and motivation,
If you do want much.

The hustle is real,
The opportunities you can bear,
Disregard the mirror in the rear,
To yourself and others, always be sincere,
Confront your fears.

The house on the hills,
What the future unveils,
Keep close of what's near.

The moochers and users,
Better know sooner.

Brush your shoulders off and ignore the hate,
Eating steak on the plate,
The perception of fate.

~Marquonda Wyatt

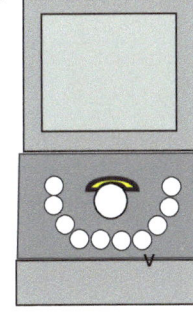

The Variations of Love

The love and affection,
The chemistry and connection,
A delicate touch on the complexion,
A very steamy session.

The crush, the touch,
Emotions initiating a reflux,
A crazy adrenaline rush.

Wine and dine,
Getting excited and nervous,
Sending chills up your spine.

Snuggle and cuddle,
The couple that makes a cute bundle,
The love will never fumble.

Love in different variations,
Does not occur on certain occasions,
The effects of elation.

The care and the warmth,
The bond can't be torn,
Trust is frequently sworn.

A love so sweet,
It can't be beat,
It will knock you off your feet,
Quality is what you seek.

A lovely romance,
The ultimate clash,
Have you doing a dance.

One of the greatest love of all,
Loving yourself and you're on the ball.

But that's not all,
The greatest love of all.
Is from the Mighty Lord above,
He provides you with the strength to stand tall.

Aside from the romance,
A lovely turtle dove.

~Marquonda Wyatt

The End

Credits and Copyrights

Copyright © 2022 Marquonda Wyatt

All rights reserved. No part of this publication may be reproduced, distributed, transferred, or transmitted in any form whatsoever, including the recording, mechanical, manual, or electronic methodologies, photocopying without the prior permission of the publisher except in the contribution of forming a review and particular alternative uses that are noncommercial permitted by the copyright law. For permission to request usage, it is crucial to write to the author and/or publisher.

Please be informed that any references to relative, historical settings, real people, and places are produced from the Author's imagination.

ISBN: 9798361723454

Author, written, and illustrated by: Marquonda Wyatt
Graphics by: Marquonda Wyatt
Publisher: Wyatt's Creative Works ™

www.ingramcontent.com/pod-product-compliance
Lightning Source LLC
Chambersburg PA
CBHW041200290426
44109CB00002B/84